Mollie Jean Scores Her First Goal

Michael Barr

Dedication

Mollie Jean Scores Her First Goal is dedicated to teachers and coaches who make learning fun. I sometimes put too much pressure on my own children playing soccer.

Acknowledgment

I want to recognize all the individuals I met who have brought soccer to the youth in American cities. They realize that the cost of playing soccer often prevents lower-income children and their families from experiencing the joy and excitement of soccer. Through their efforts, these children are now given the opportunity to meet success and gain new opportunities through the game.

About the Author

Michael Barr is well-known in the soccer world. He has received numerous awards from the United States Soccer community as well as hall of fame status in high school, college, and the state of Pennsylvania. He has been a featured speaker and instructor at United Soccer Coaches Conventions. He has written numerous articles on coaching soccer as the Director of Coaching for Eastern Pennsylvania for 18 years. He has taught US Soccer Coaching Licenses throughout the country for the past thirty-five years.

In addition to coaching soccer, he was a special education teacher working with students from elementary school through high school.

Michael and his wife Barbara have four wonderful children and nine grandchildren.

Page Blank Intentionally

No cartoons and Disney movies for me! I was awake before my mom and dad and quickly woke the others. Saturday was my favorite day because I played soccer.

My mother helped me with my shin guards and socks. I pulled the laces of my soccer shoes real tight. I wondered, as my last bow was tied, would this be the day I finally scored a goal?

My brother Aidan got my water bottle, and we walked towards our car. My sister Emma sat next to me in the middle of the back seat as I found a seat near the window.

Through the car window, I began to see the soccer field. The yellow net on the goals and the fresh white lines of the field appeared to be a giant invitation to welcome me to my soccer game.

I was early for my game, so I practiced passing with my brother.

"Use the inside of both of your feet when you pass, Mollie," shouted Aidan.

Sometimes, I forgot and used only my right foot.

Before Coach Jones got to the field, members of my team sometimes pushed each other and did not pay attention, but when he called us together, everyone listened and got ready to play.

All of us brought our own balls for our warm-up, and as if by magic, we began to move with the ball at our feet.

"Touch with the inside, outside, and sole of your foot," Coach Jones commanded.

The ball seemed to be part of me as we moved to his every word. I tried to imagine myself dribbling by a defender and finally scoring my first goal.

My coach said, "Dribble with just your left foot."

My daydream ended in a thud as I tripped over the ball. I was dynamite dribbling with my right foot, but I was not so hot with my left.

As I was slowly getting up, my coach whispered to me, "Don't worry, Mollie. When you least expect it, your left foot will work just fine."

The referee, wearing an orange shirt and black shorts, blew his whistle. Only seven players played at one time for each team. I liked to play on the outside. There was always plenty of space by the touchline to dribble and run by defenders.

Abigail was the best player on my team. She was bigger and faster than I was. She scored a lot of goals and had the hardest shot on the team. Maybe her shot would rub off on me, and I would get a chance to high-five with all the players on my team.

From the beginning, the game was fast and furious. I couldn't help but notice the red cheeks of the parents as they shouted instructions, which many of us never heard. I just listened to my coach and tried my best.

Billy Franklin was my friend from school and on my team. He was a little overweight, and he told me before the game, "I wish I were home riding my bike instead of playing soccer."

I couldn't blame him; his father was always yelling at Billy. We sometimes called his dad "Mr. Work Harder." All he ever said to Billy was, "Work harder! Work harder!"

Of course, Abigail scored the first goal. The ball seemed to be in the goal before the keeper had his hands up. She walked back to midfield with her right hand high as the rest of us jumped to slap her hand and congratulate her for her goal.

We had a 1-0 lead, and I rested the last ten minutes of the first half. I was not very tired, but instead of running around the sidelines with my friends, I sat on a ball and watched the game.

At halftime, the parents usually brought oranges, but last week, Kristen was stung by a bee. We only drank water now.

The second half had a slow start. Throw-in after throw-in was called as the ball banged off our shins and across the touchlines. Sometimes, it was hard to get the ball from one side to the other. Sometimes, we couldn't even keep the ball on the field.

Melissa's dad from the other team screamed, "Concentrate," but I wasn't sure what concentrate meant.

The other team was not as strong as my team, but they did have a boy named Shane who was bigger than all of us, even Abigail! I sometimes turned my back when I thought Shane and I would collide. My coach and my dad told me not to be afraid, but they were not staring at Shane's belly button when that collision was about to take place!

With only five minutes left in the game, Shane kicked the ball, and it seemed to go a mile in the sky! Every player on both teams stopped playing and watched as the ball got smaller as it moved higher. It appeared to stay up forever, but slowly, almost like a balloon, it began to come down. I was worried and shouted at our goalkeeper Carlos, because the ball was heading right for the goal we were defending.

Carlos began moving back and forth in front of the goal with his hands held high in the air.

I could almost imagine Carlos in the middle of a lake, trying to walk from one end of a big rowboat to the other end as he followed his target in the sky.

Carlos wobbled and then fell. I could almost hear a splash when his body hit the ground. Uh-oh, the ball was still falling, and poor Carlos could only gaze at the clouds as the ball came to earth and nestled itself in the corner of the goal.

Shane raised his arms and waited for his team to run toward him for the usual hugs, high-fives, and congratulations. Parents from the other team were jumping up and down, clapping. Our fans were shouting for one more goal. All it took was one big kick from Shane to make both sides active behind the touchlines.

The referee's whistle telling us to kick off did not quiet the noise from the parents. Shouts of encouragement were coming from both sides as the game entered the final minutes. The ball moved from one end of the field to the other as if it were on a yo-yo. The other team had Shane all the way in the back, and he cleared the ball every time we got near his team's goal. Even Abigail could not get by Shane. I began to think a tie wasn't so bad.

Abigail, Shane, and my friend Billy gathered to collect a bouncing ball at midfield. Strangely, all three of the players bumped into each other, tumbled, and fell to the ground. The ball just lay there as I sprinted nervously towards it.

Just as I reached the ball, Shane's foot caught my back foot. The ball was rolling in the direction of the goal, and suddenly, I found myself flying completely out of control. The ball no longer seemed so important. I was just hoping for a soft landing.

My landing was smooth, but I had to think fast. Their keeper sprinted out, and I immediately cut the ball to my left foot. "All those dribbling exercises do pay off," I thought to myself.

I saw the goal and took a shot with my left foot. The laces of my left shoe went directly through the center of the ball, and it seemed to jump off my foot. Luckily, it zoomed toward the goal.

The back of the net jumped, and the ball lazily came to rest in the goal. From the back, I heard the referee's final whistle.

I peeked back toward midfield and saw Billy still on the ground. His elbows and hands were supporting a face with a huge smile. I reached down and tried to pull Billy to his feet, but he was too heavy, and I fell on top of him.

We were both laughing as I said to Billy, "I scored the winning goal, but you get the assist."

My whole team ran up to hug me, and I saw my parents jumping up and down. What a wonderful feeling!

Both teams always enjoyed lining up, slapping hands, and saying, "Good game!" but this time was the best. I scored my first goal, and it turned out to be the winning goal.

I walked to the sidelines, and as my mom squeezed me tightly,

I noticed "Mr. Work Harder" give Billy a big hug, too.